Tracing

Your tract!

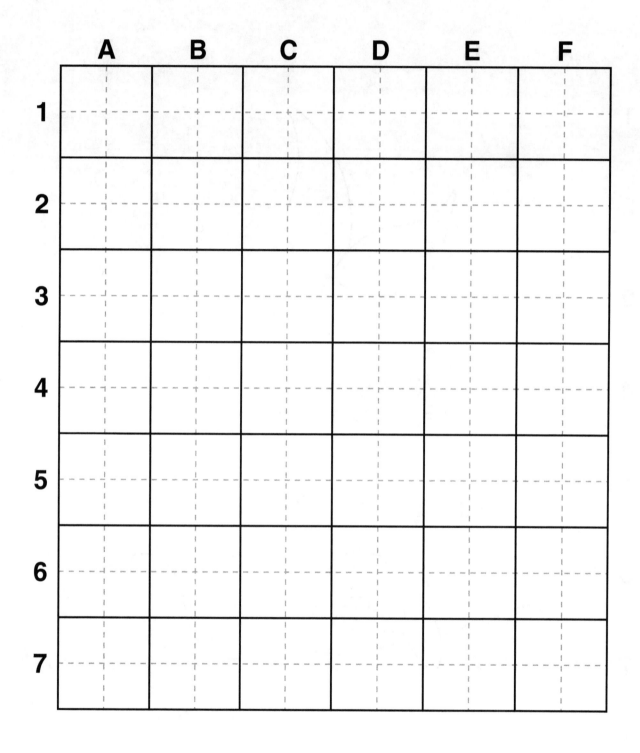

Coloring

Practice!

Make perfect!

Tracing

Your tract!

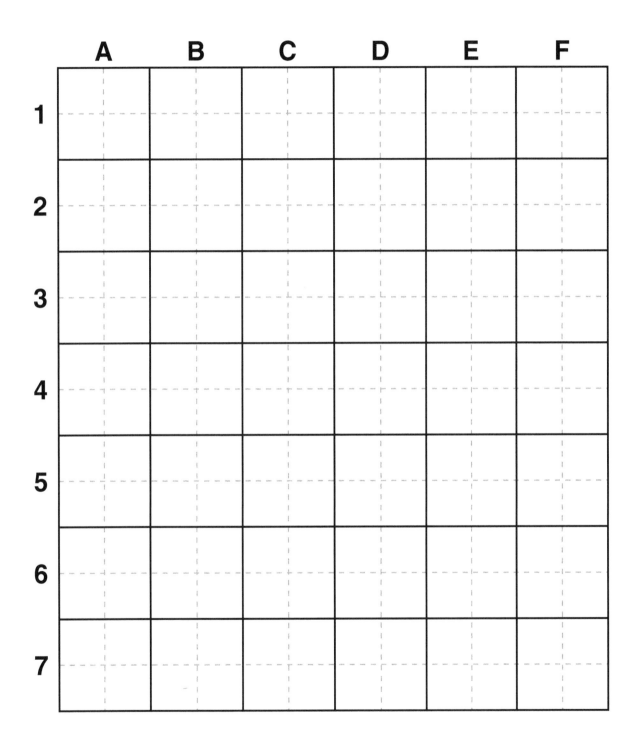

Coloring

Practice!

Make perfect!

Tracing

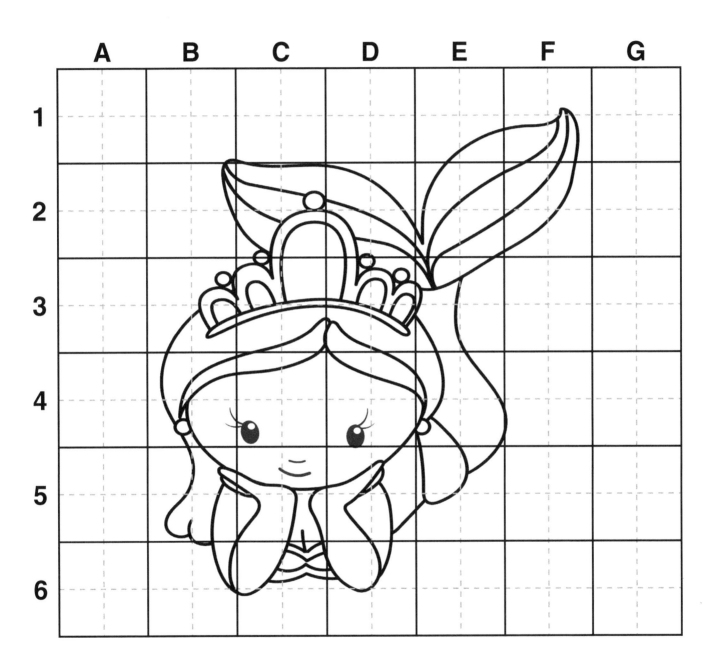

Your tract!

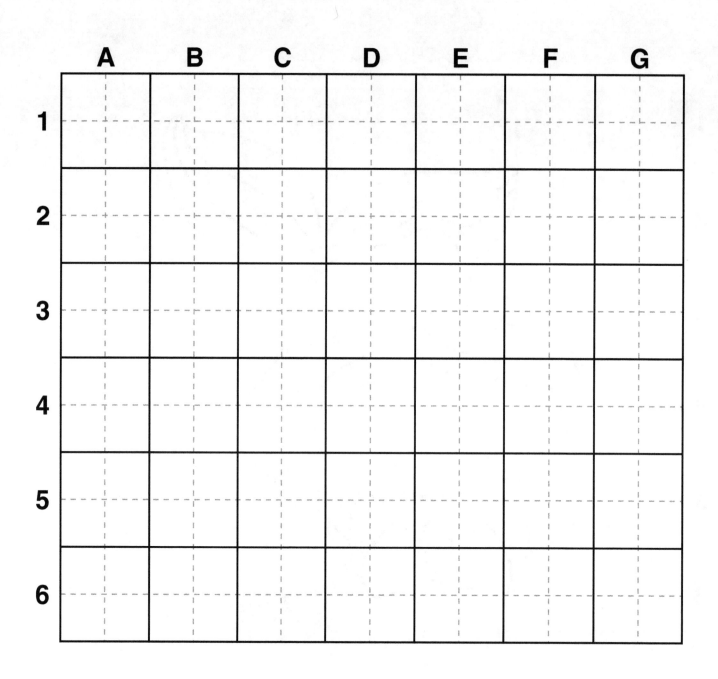

Coloring

Practice!

Make perfect!

Tracing

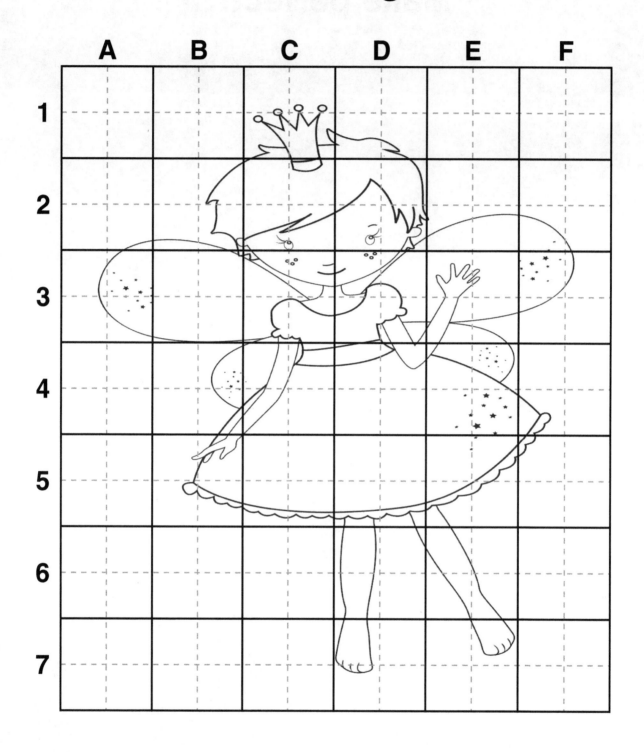

Your tract!

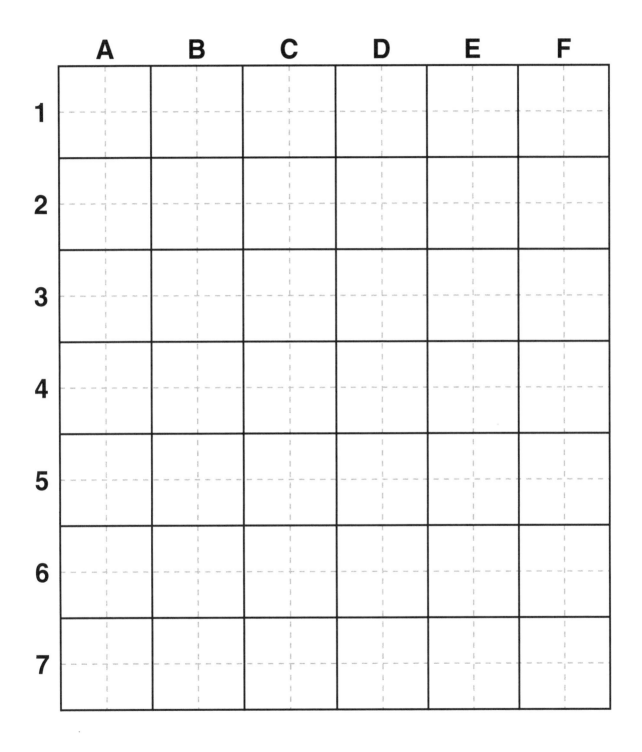

Coloring

Practice!

Make perfect!

Tracing

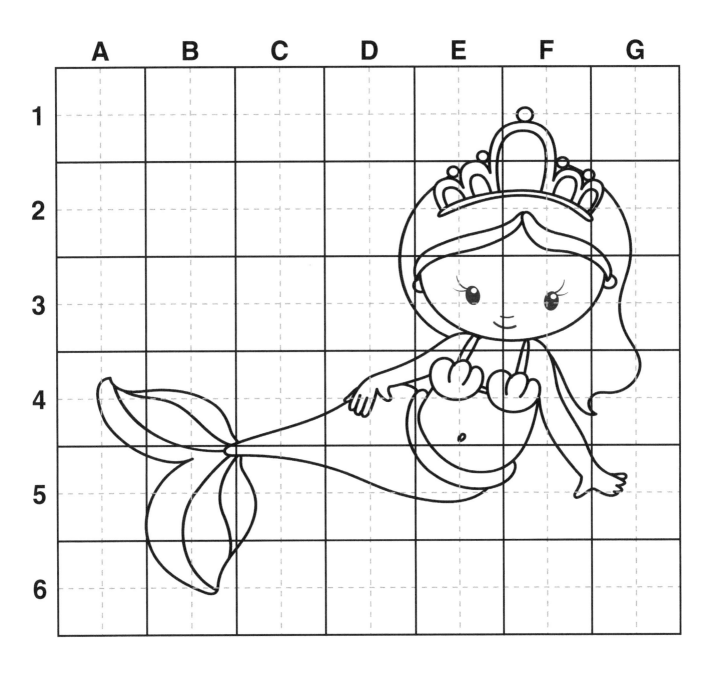

Your tract!

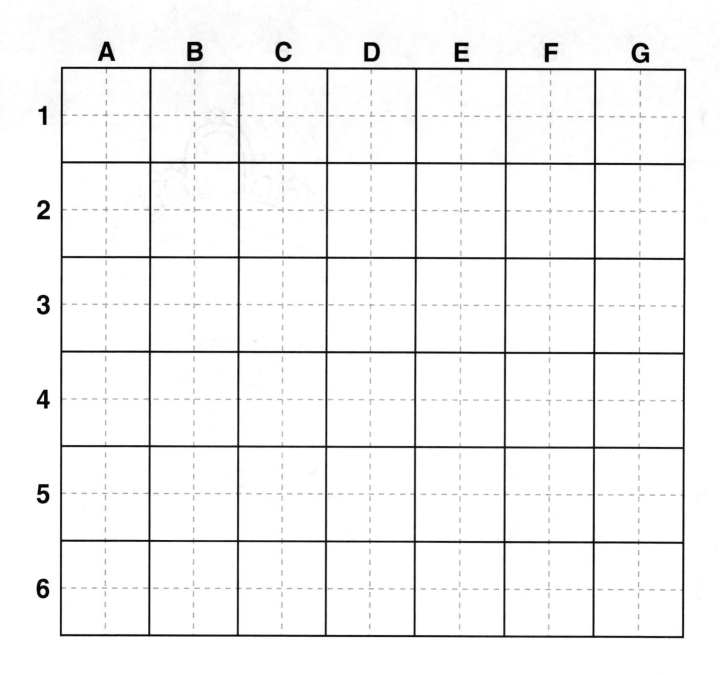

Coloring

Practice!

Make perfect!

Tracing

Your tract!

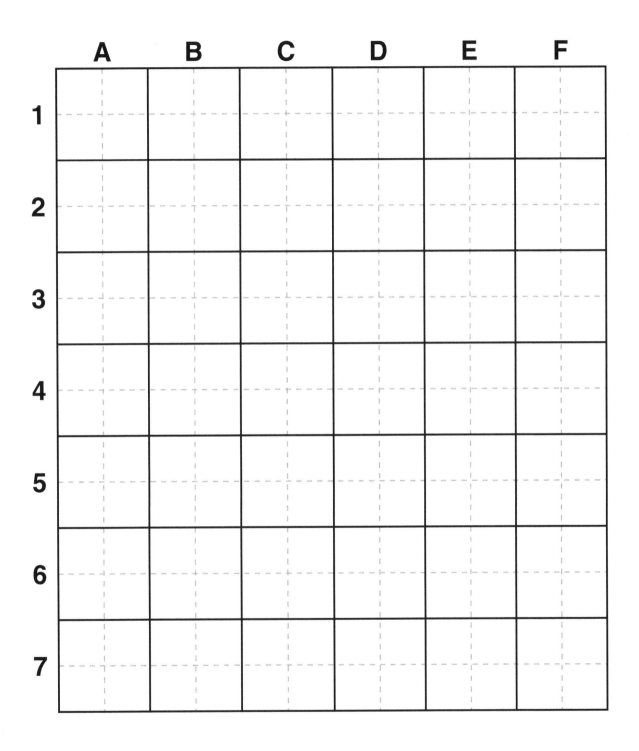

Coloring

Practice!

Make perfect!

Tracing

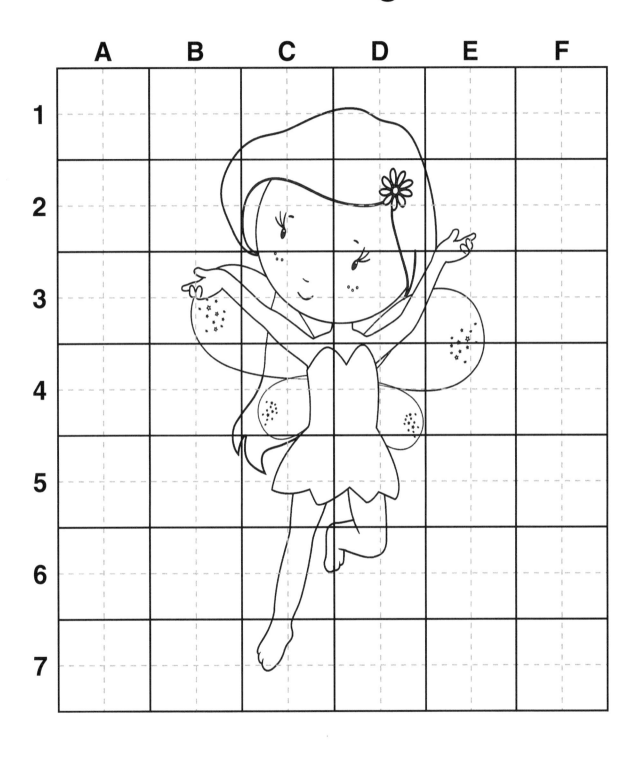

Your tract!

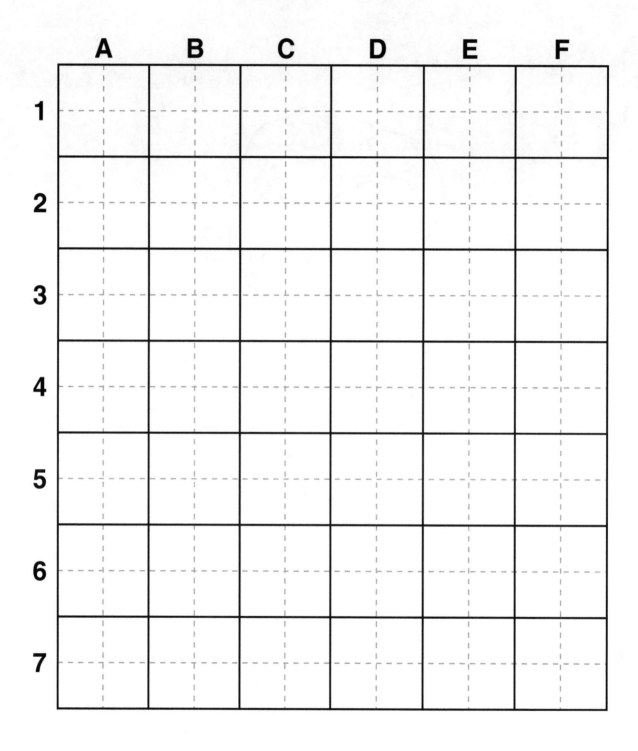

Coloring

Practice!

Make perfect!

Tracing

Your tract!

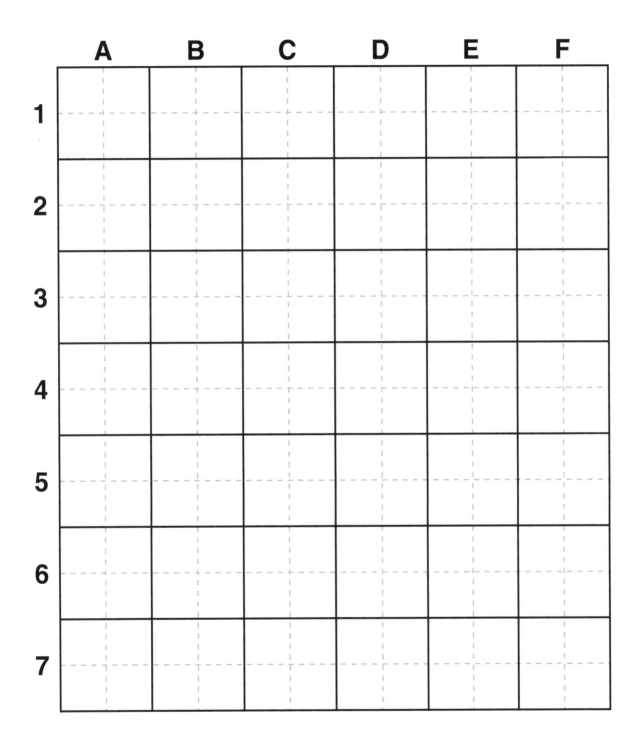

Coloring

Practice!

Make perfect!

Tracing

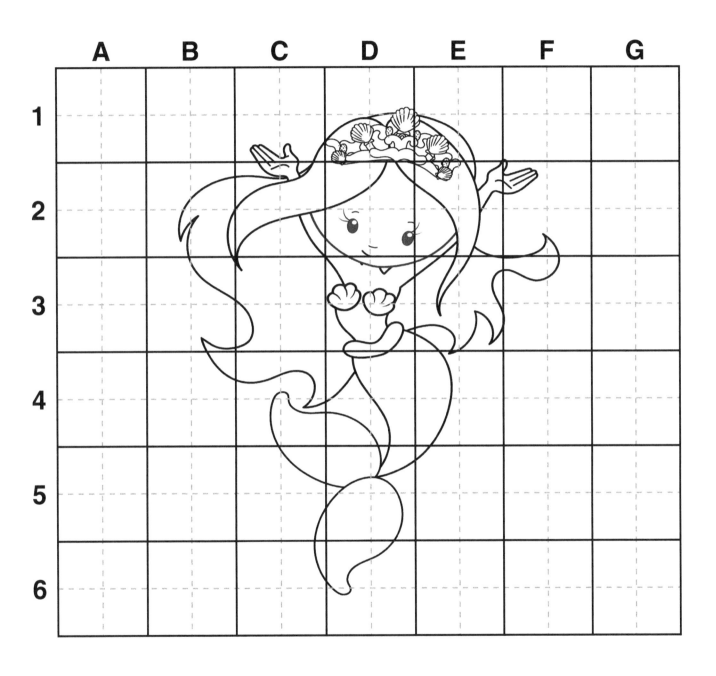

Your tract!

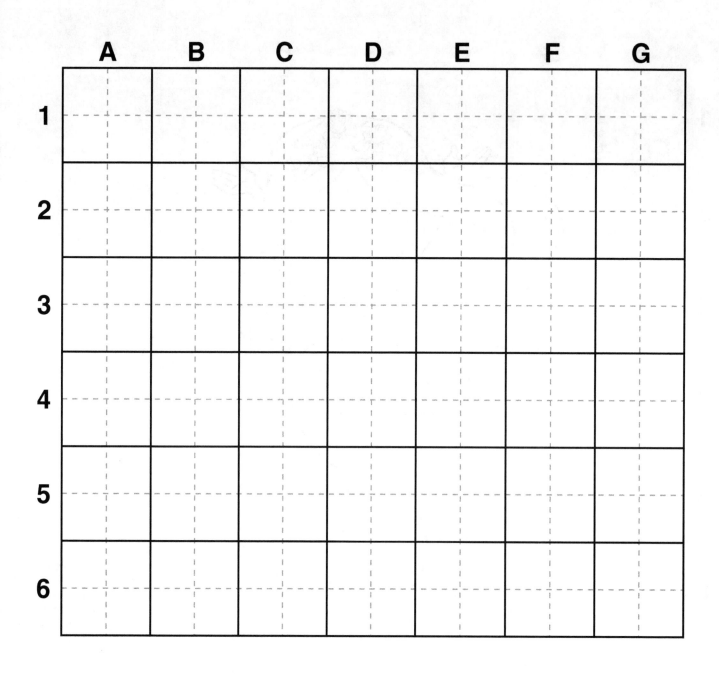

Coloring

Practice!

Make perfect!

Tracing

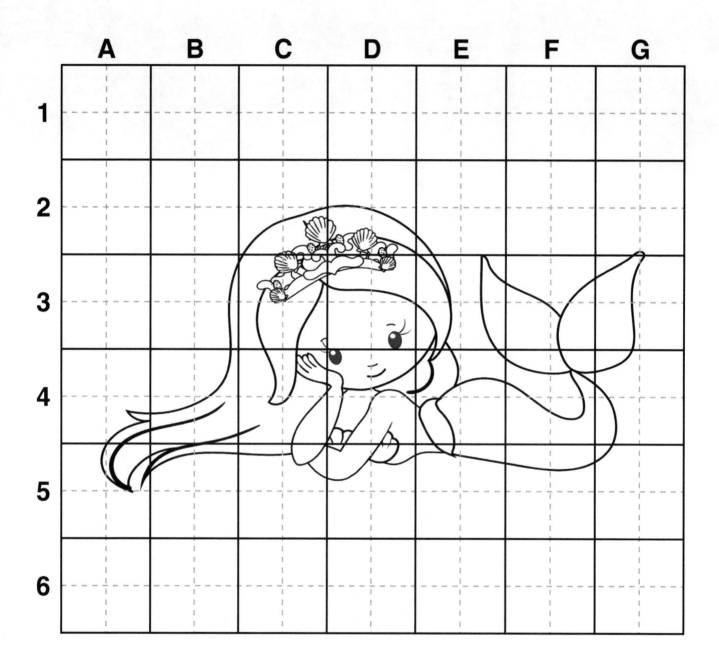

Your tract!

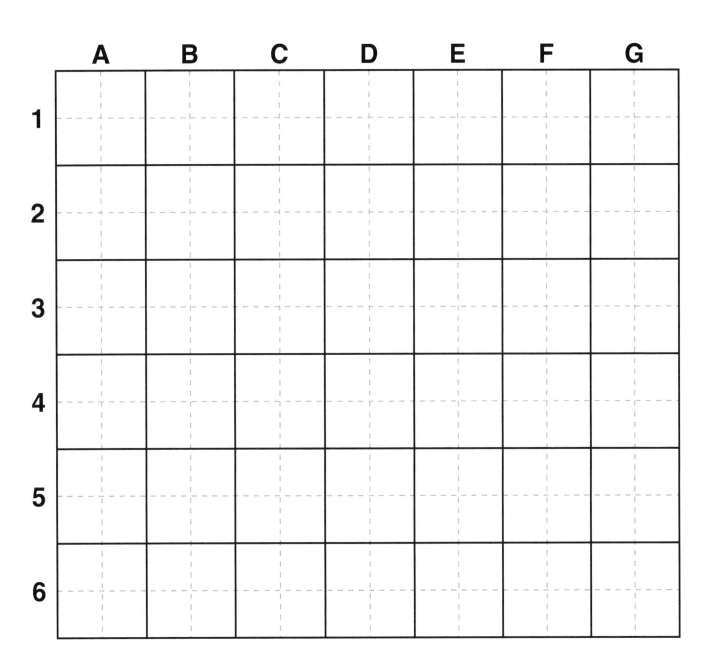

Coloring

Practice!

Make perfect!

Tracing

Your tract!

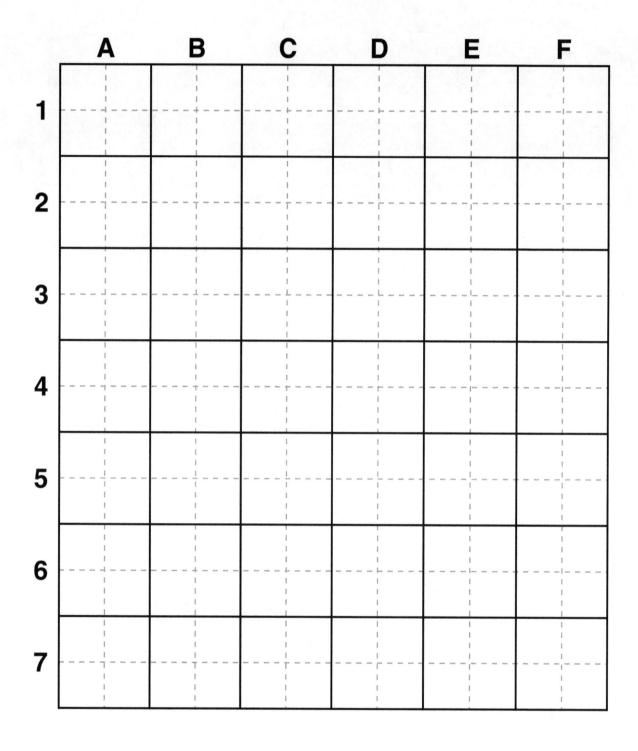

Coloring

Practice!

Make perfect!

Tracing

Your tract!

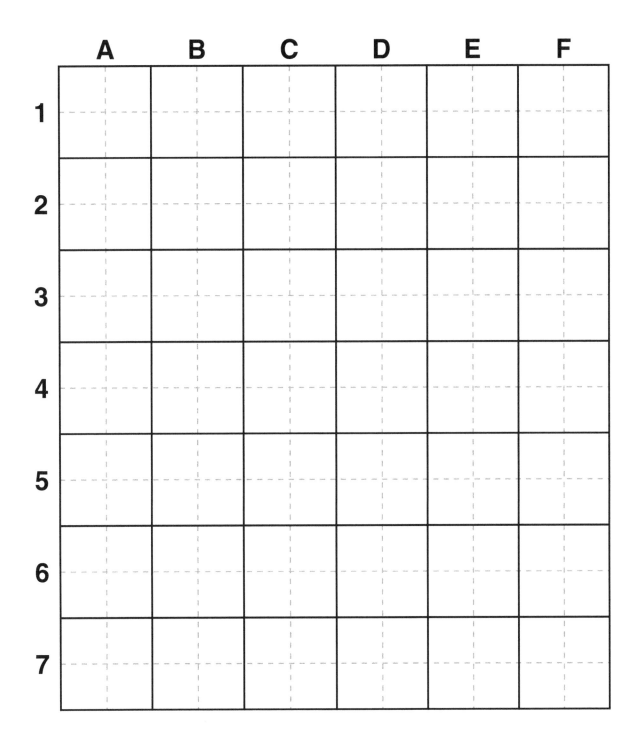

Coloring

Practice!

Make perfect!

Tracing

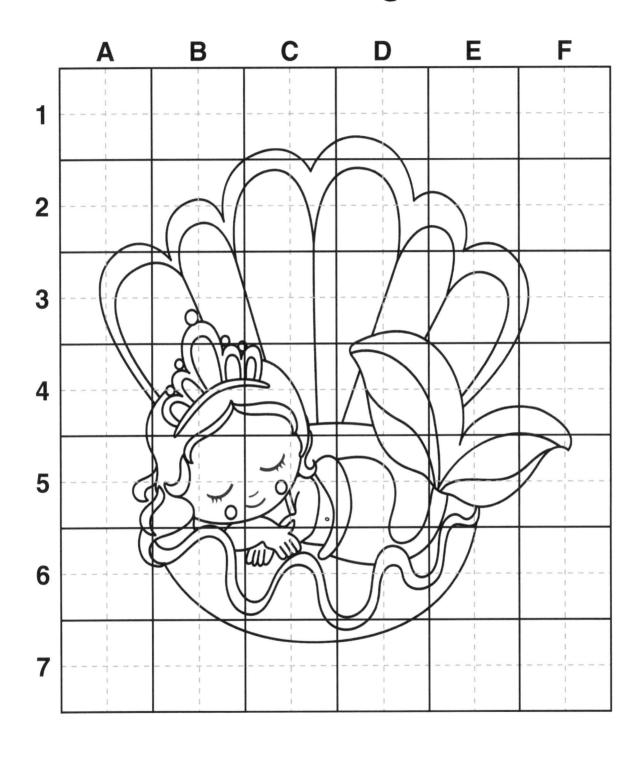

Your tract!

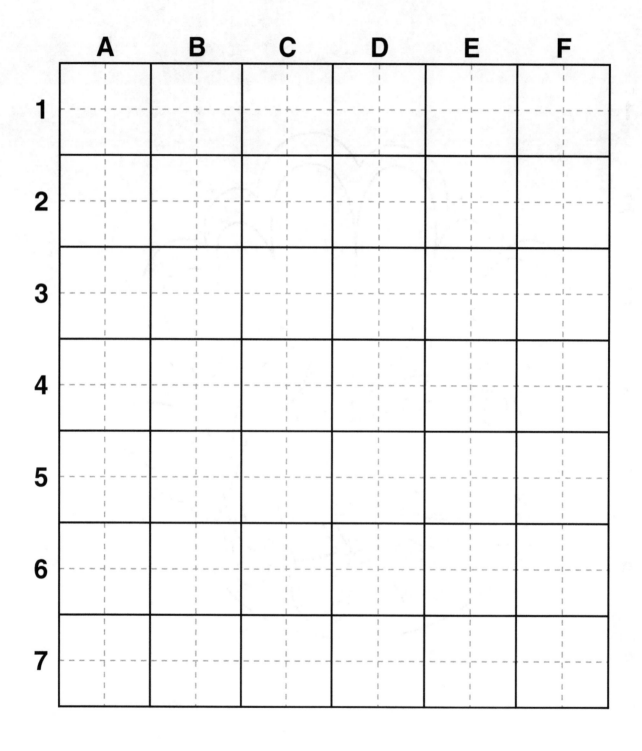

Coloring

Practice!

Make perfect!

Tracing

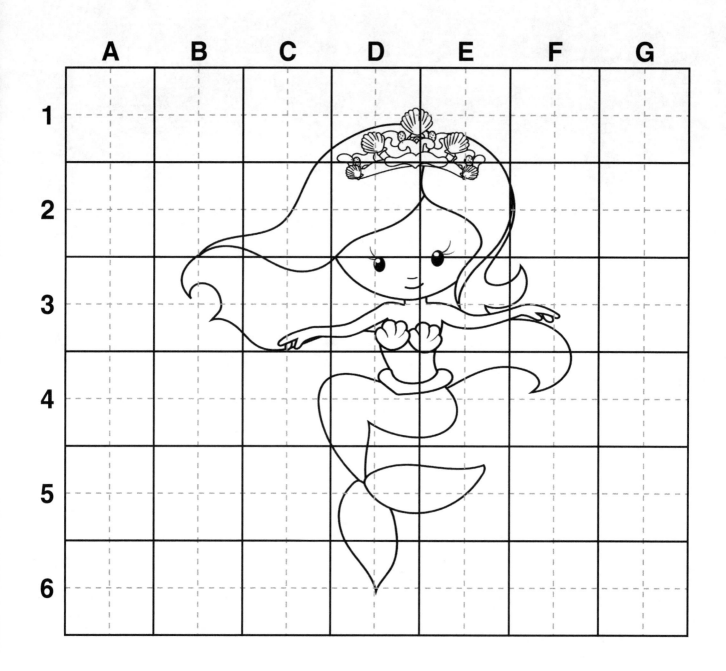

Your tract!

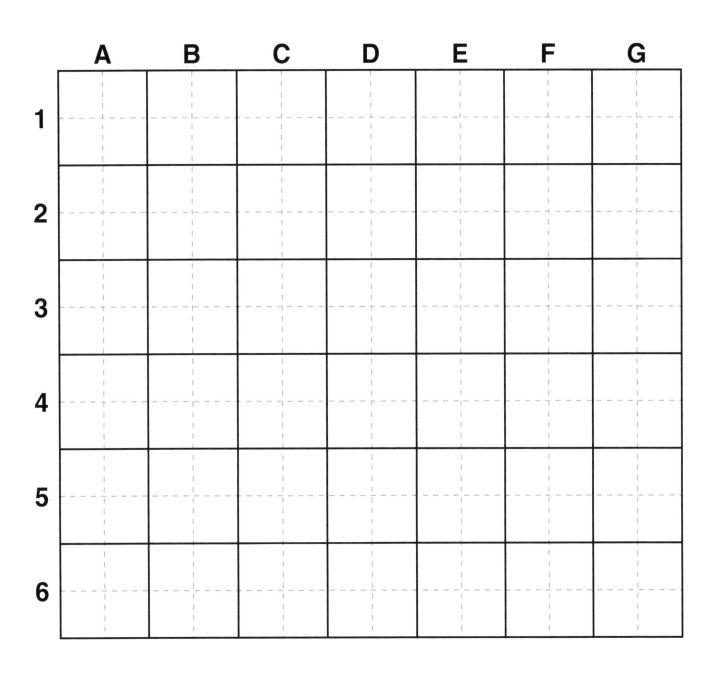

Coloring

Practice!

Make perfect!

Tracing

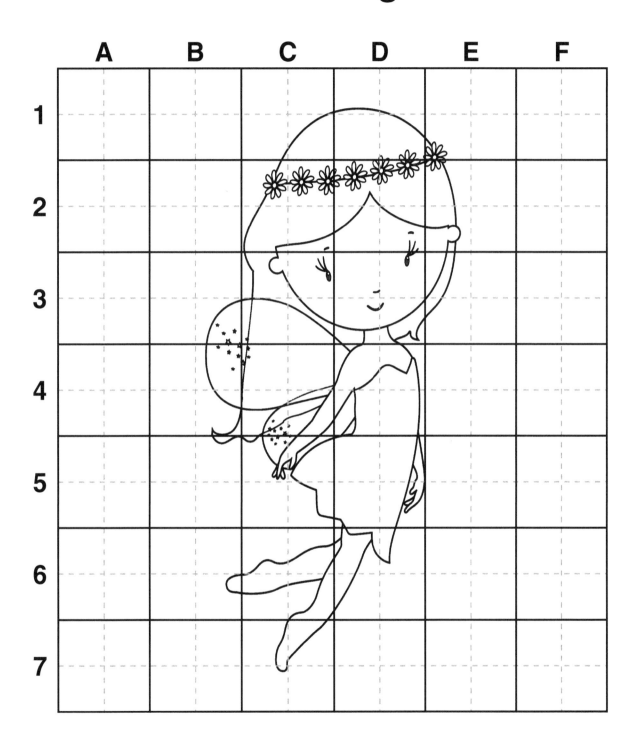

Your tract!

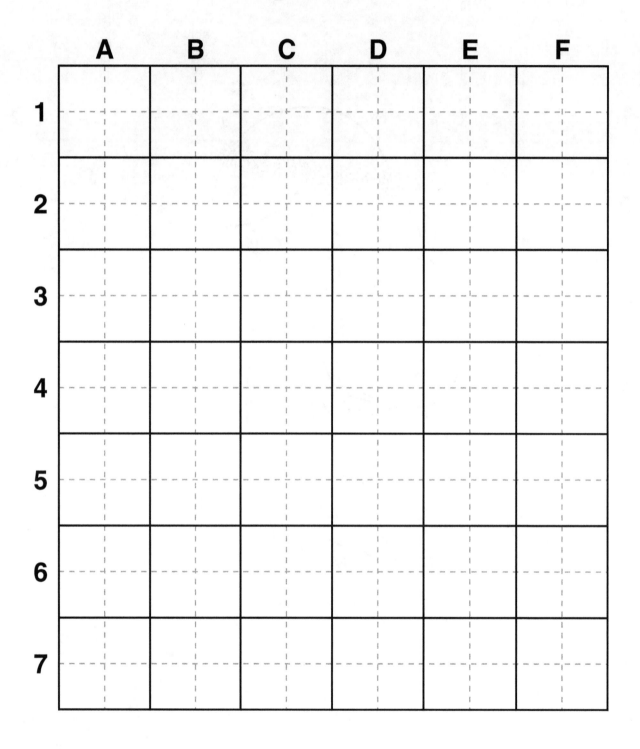

Coloring

Practice!

Make perfect!

Tracing

Your tract!

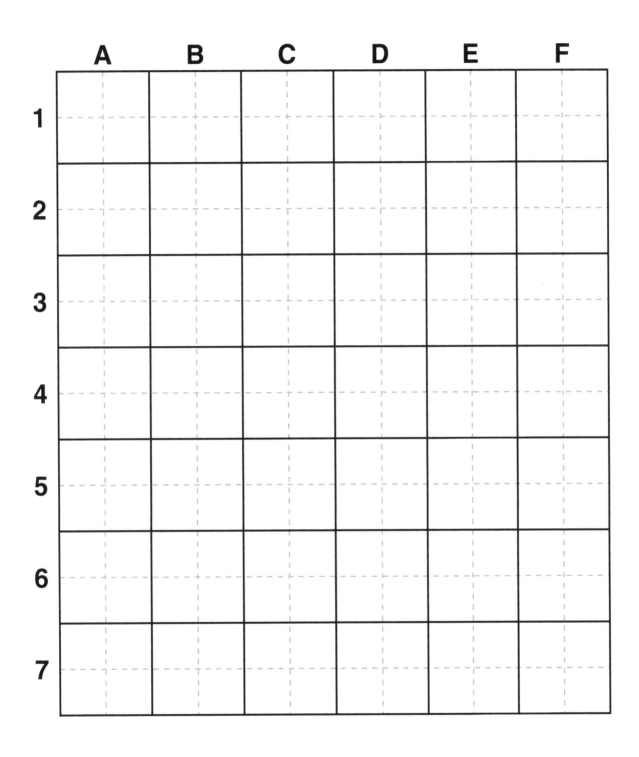

Coloring

Practice!

Make perfect!

Tracing

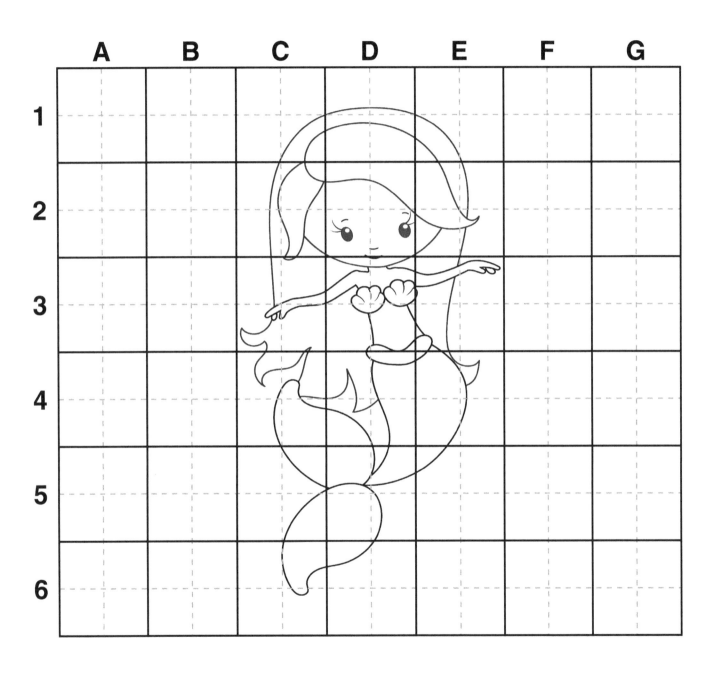

Your tract!

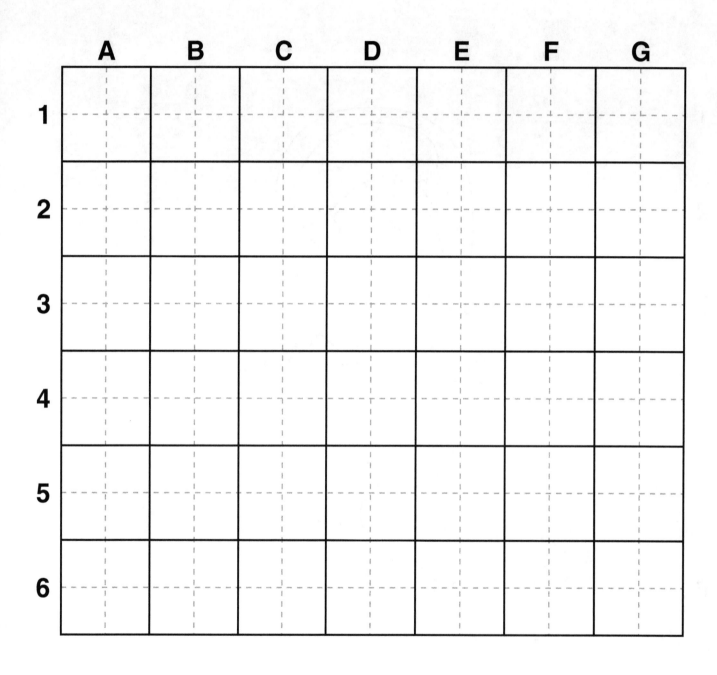

Coloring

Practice!

Make perfect!

Tracing

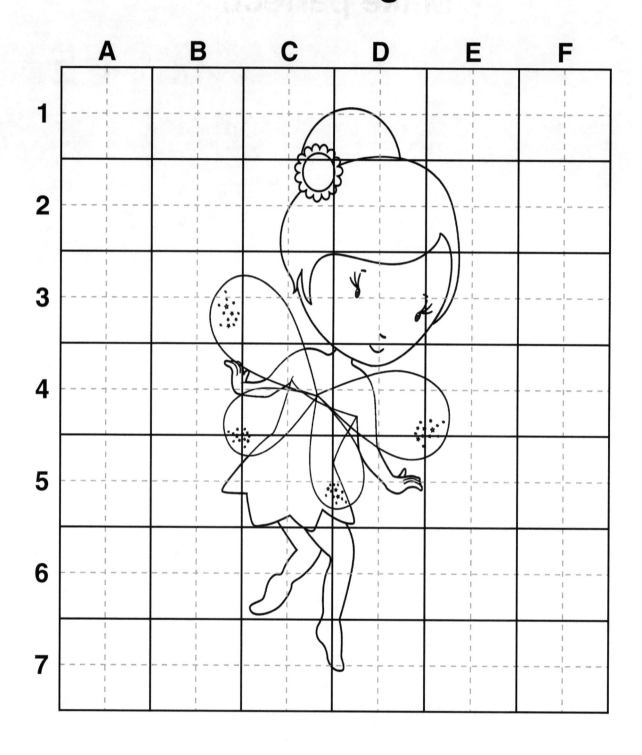

Your tract!

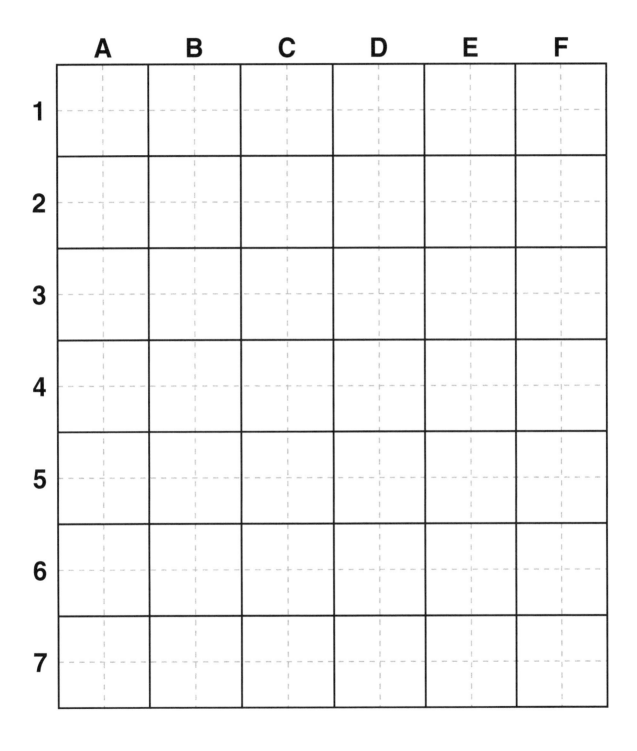

Coloring

Practice!

Make perfect!

Tracing

Your tract!

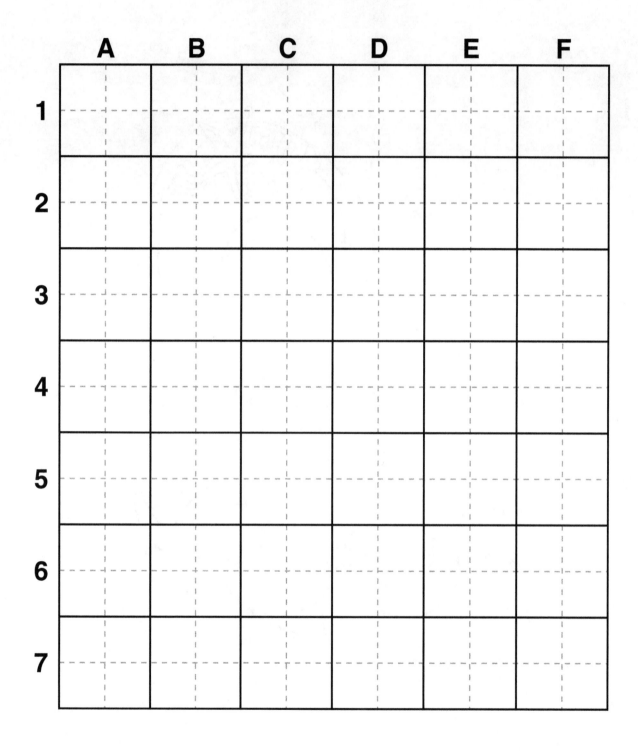

Coloring

Practice!

Make perfect!

Tracing

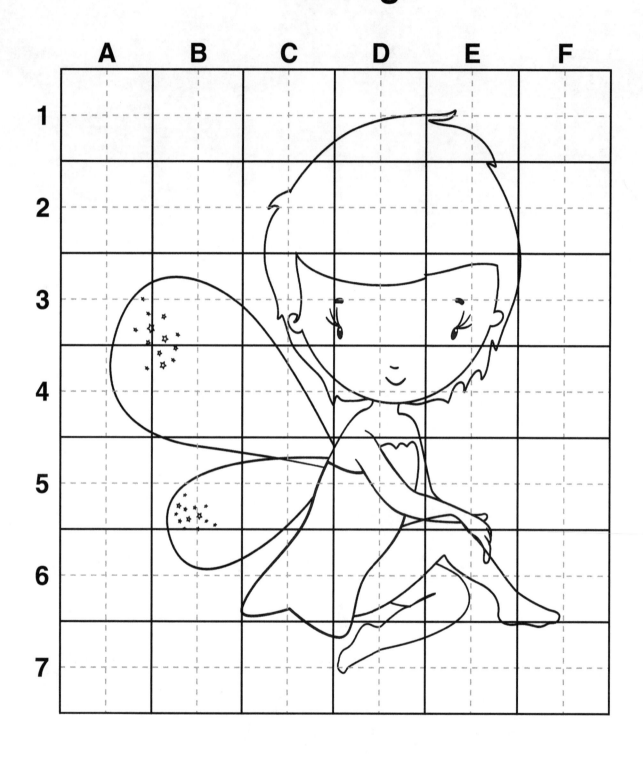

Your tract!

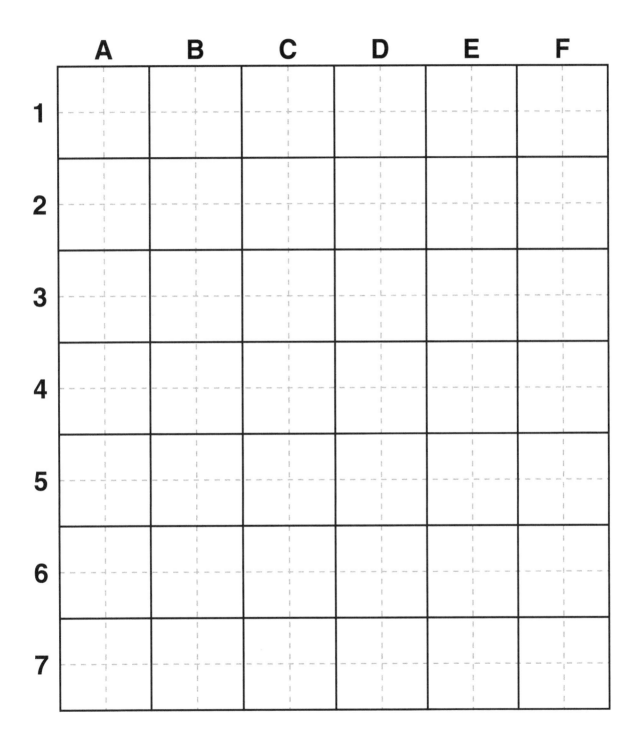

Coloring

Practice!

Make perfect!

Tracing

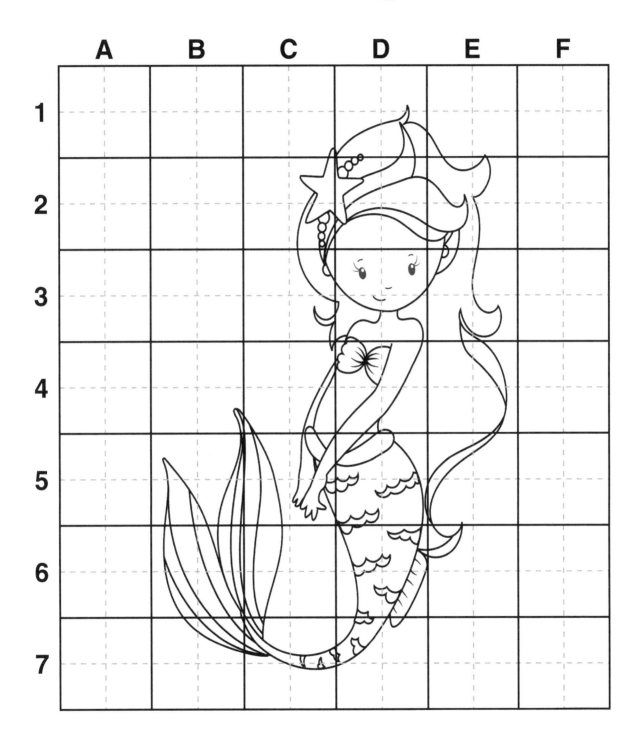

Your tract!

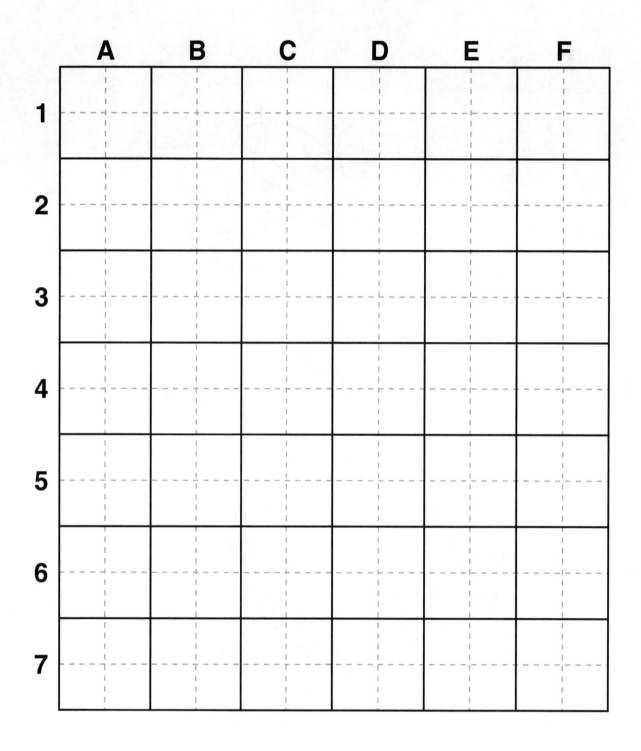

Coloring

Practice!

Make perfect!

Tracing

Your tract!

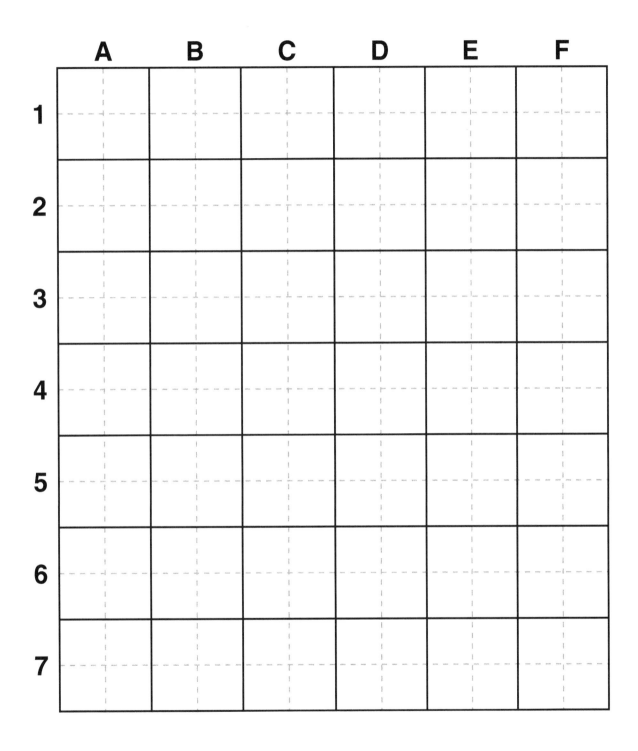

Coloring

Practice!

Make perfect!

Tracing

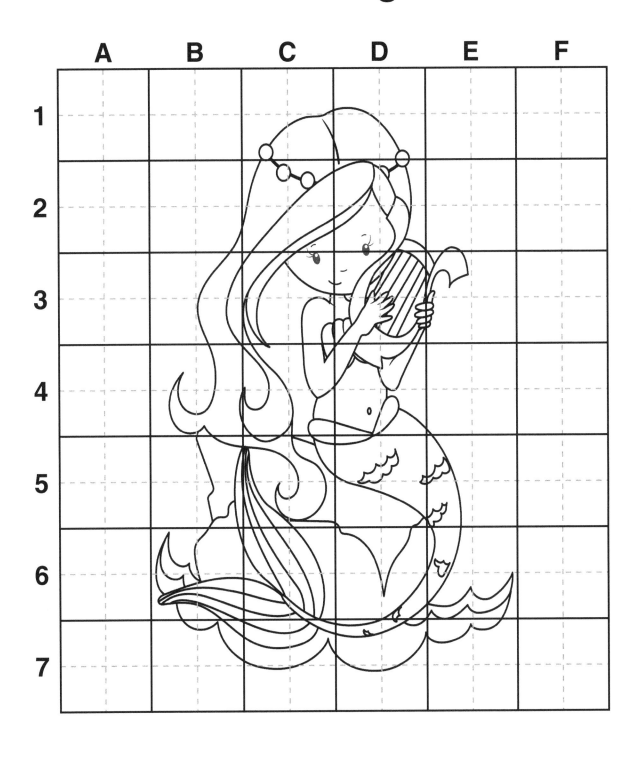

Your tract!

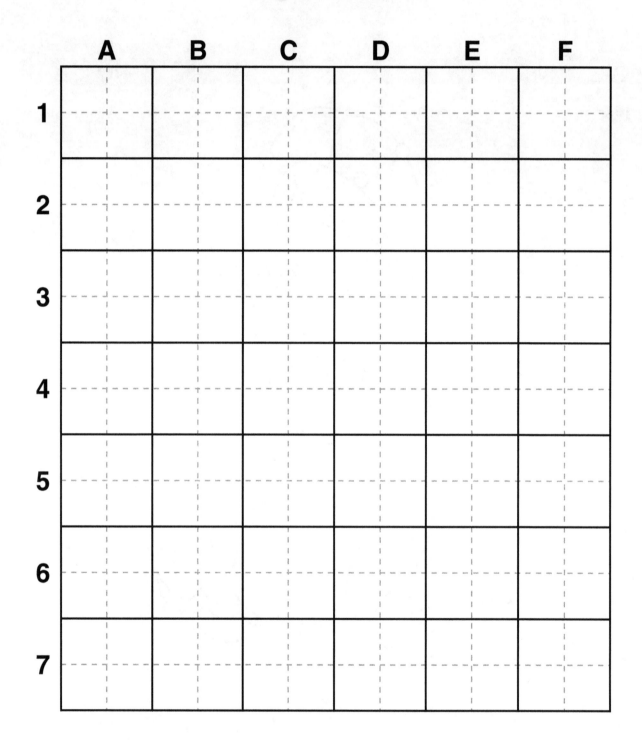

Coloring

Practice!

Make perfect!

Tracing

Your tract!

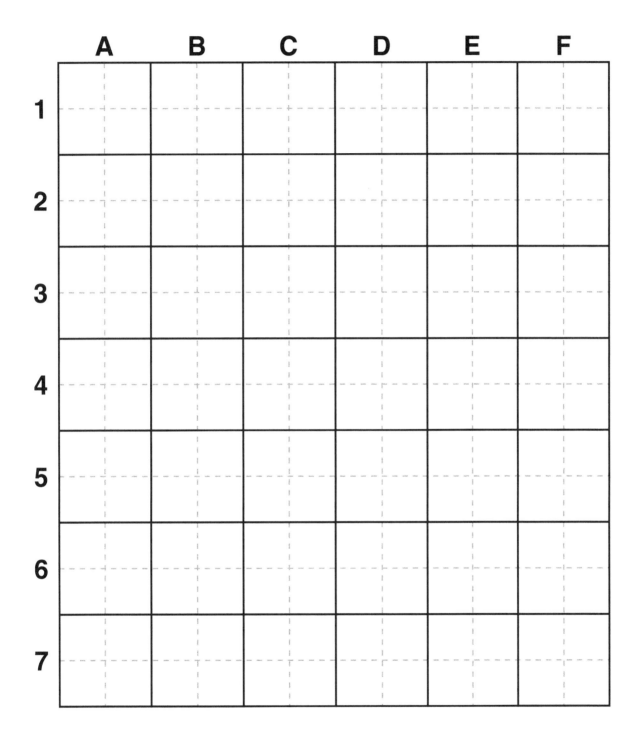

Coloring

Practice!

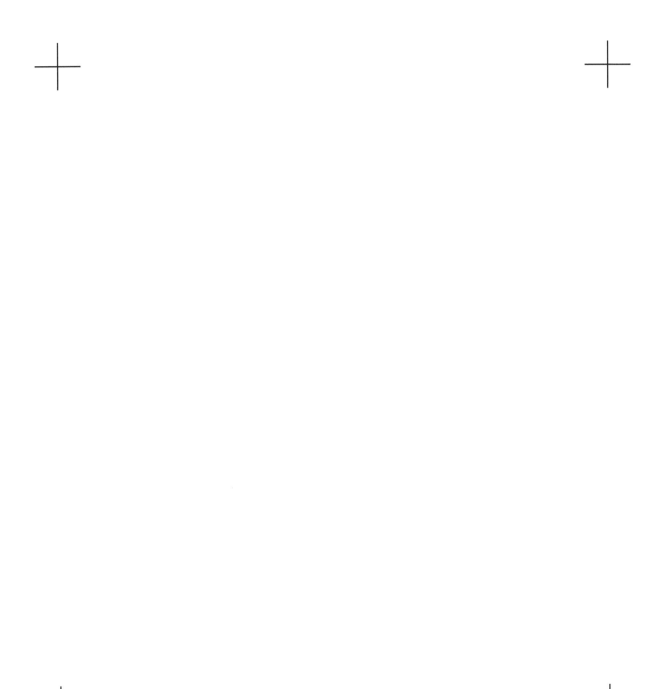

Make perfect!

Tracing

Your tract!

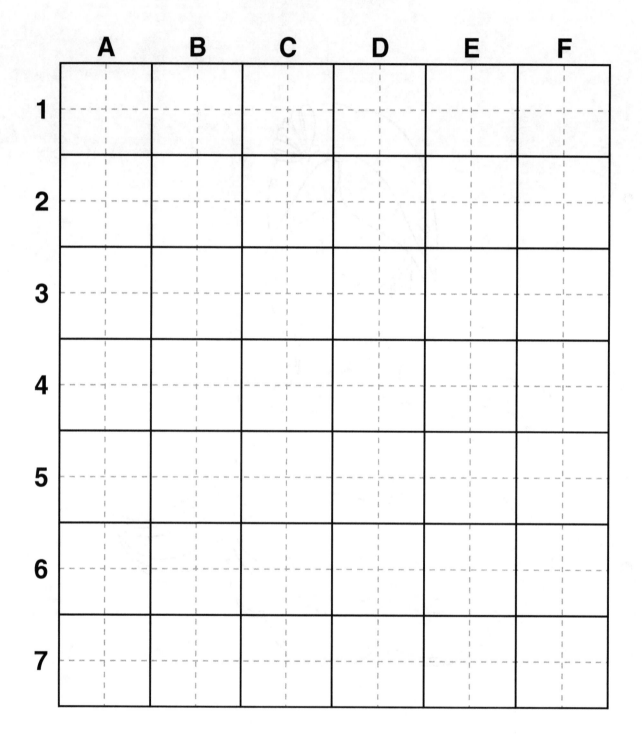

Coloring

Practice!

Make perfect!

Tracing

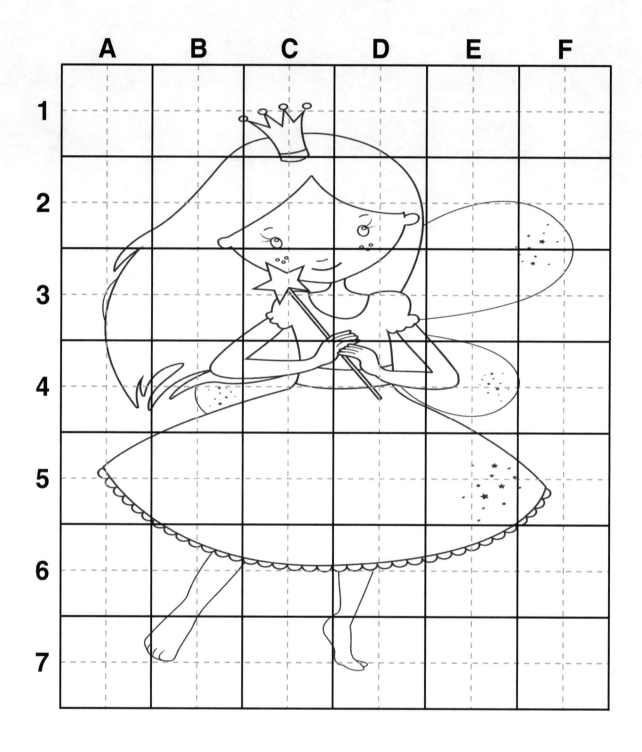

Your tract!

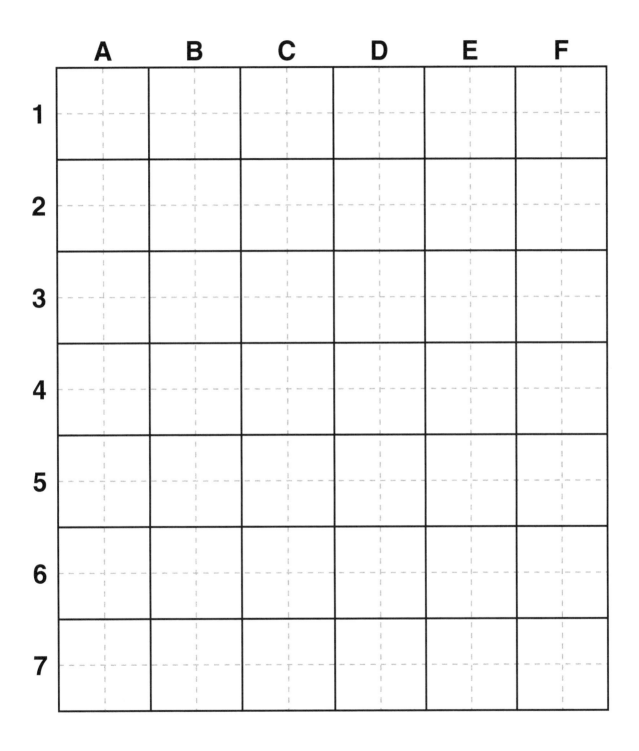

Coloring

Practice!

Make perfect!

Tracing

Your tract!

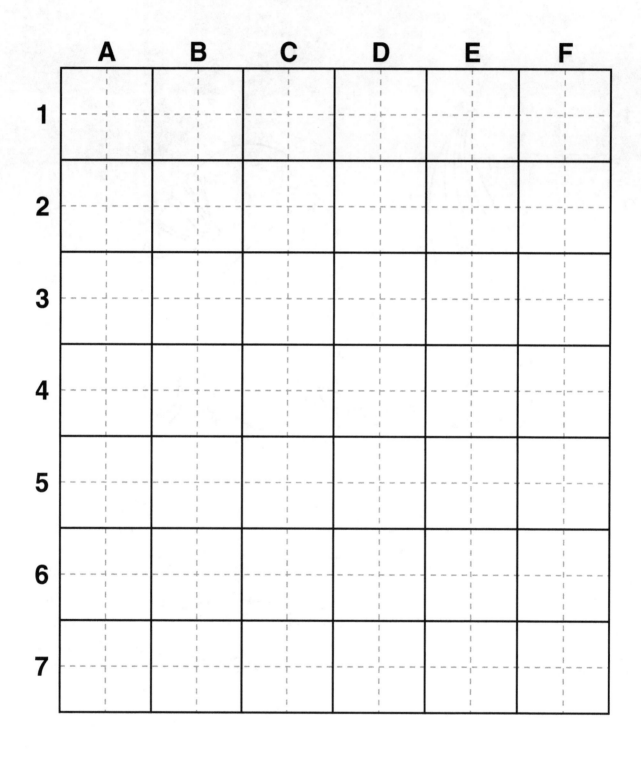

Coloring

Practice!

Make perfect!

Tracing

Your tract!

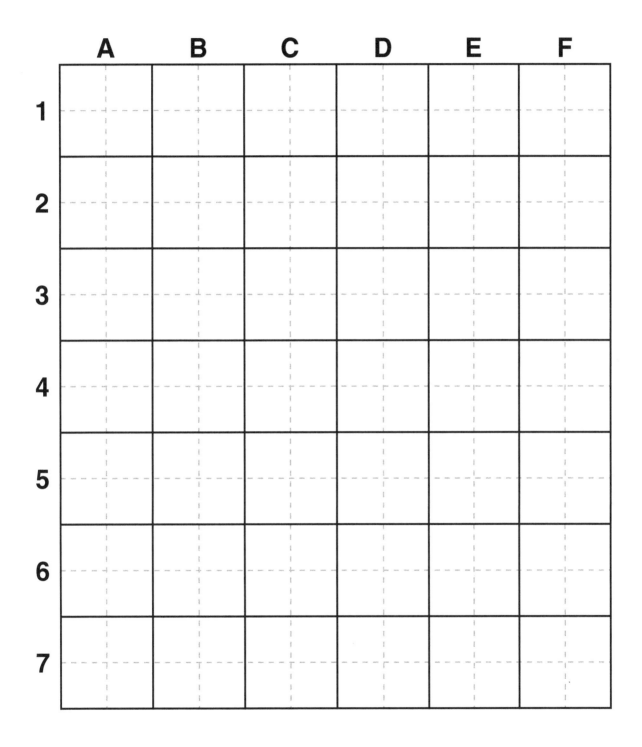

Coloring

Practice!

Make perfect!

Tracing

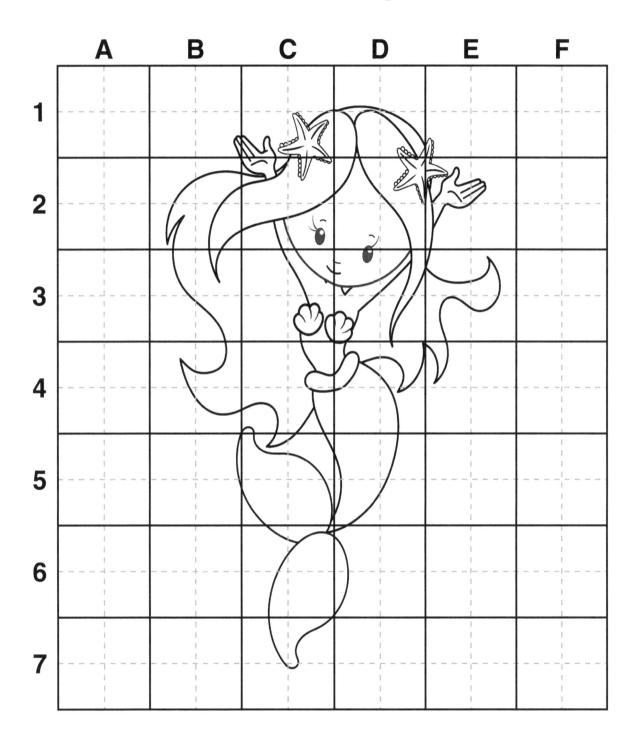

Your tract!

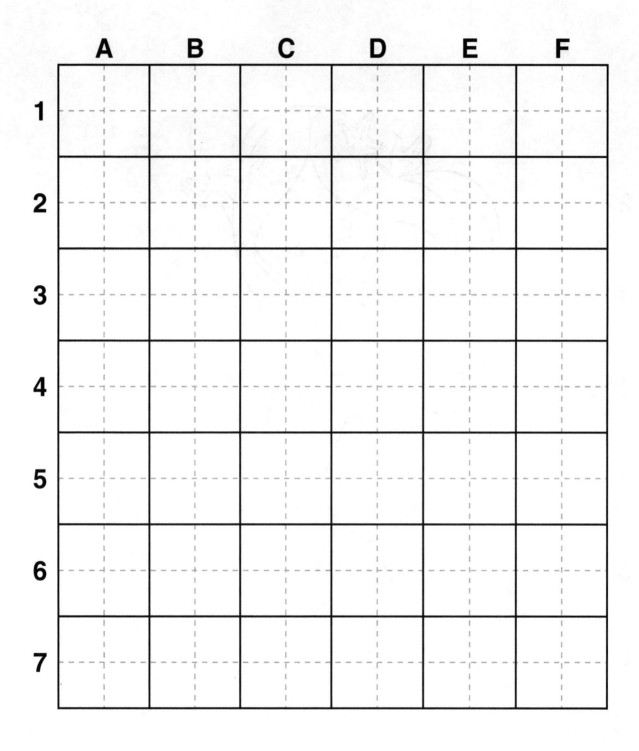

Coloring

Practice!

Make perfect!

Tracing

Your tract!

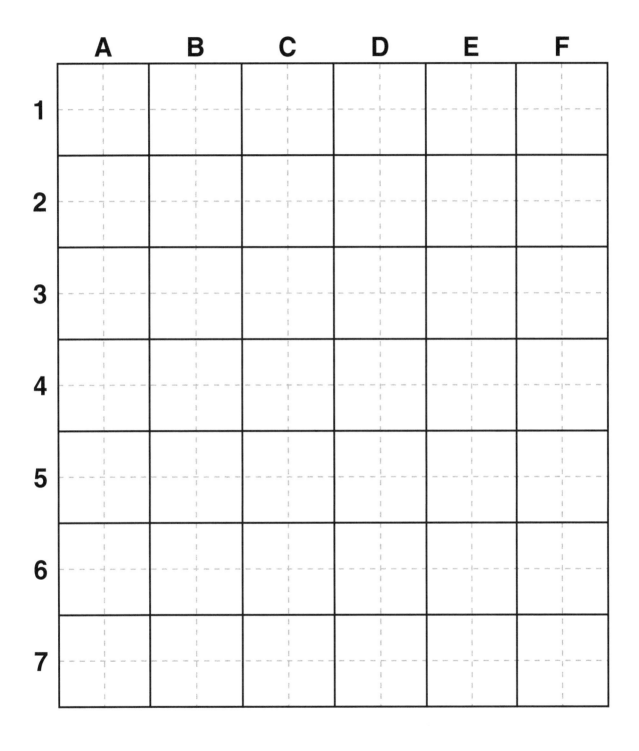

Coloring

Practice!

Make perfect!

Tracing

Your tract!

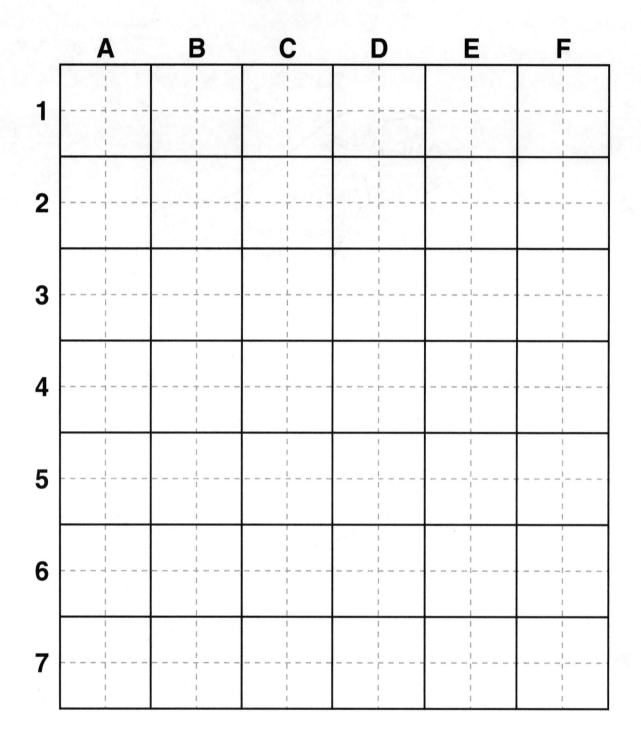

Coloring

Practice!

Make perfect!

Tracing

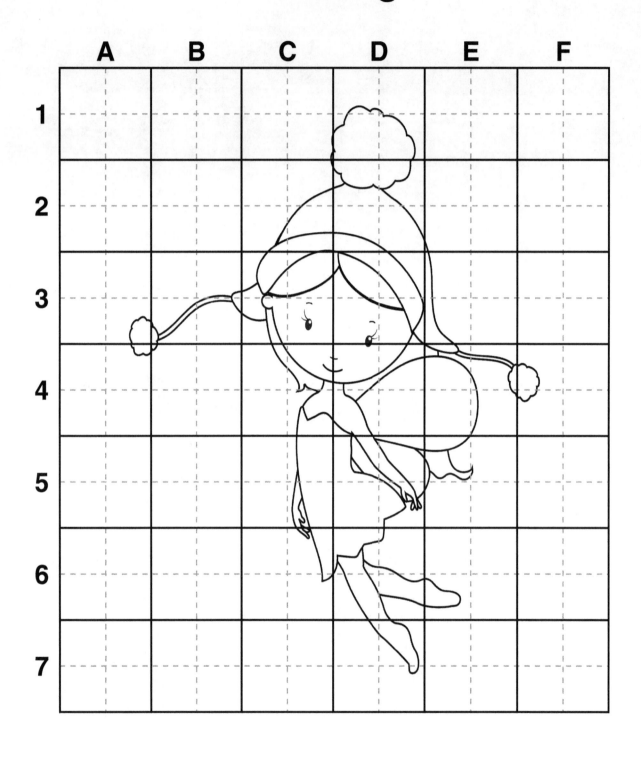

Your tract!

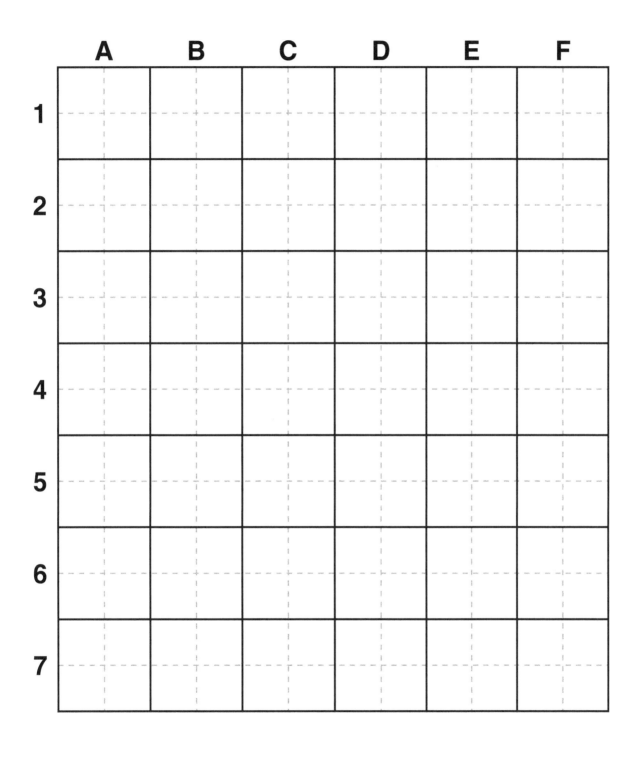

Coloring

Practice!

Make perfect!

CPSIA information can be obtained
at www.ICGtesting.com
Printed in the USA
LVHW061815281122
734200LV00034B/1743